H/ERO/T/IC BOOK

Marta Markoska

Proverse Hong Kong

2020

Macedonian writer, **MARTA MARKOSKA**, b. Skopje 1981, with a background in General and Comparative Literature and Cultural Studies, and published in these areas, is also known as an award-winning poet and short story writer. Markoska is also well known to audiences with her Late Night Show named, **Marta's Palace**, and from **The Campaign to show the Beauty of a Woman After Breast Cancer**, which she is launching at the very same time as publishing this book.

In *H/ERO/T/IC BOOK*, Macedonian writer, Marta Markoska writes about her passionate but tragically-ended story with her ex-husband, the devotion and loving support of one man, and her experiences with a few other men after her marriage ended, while she was struggling with the process of surviving breast cancer. She wrote these poems as she underwent a series of aesthetic surgeries and worked at the gym to develop her body to its best perfection. In these poems, she rediscovers herself in her altered body, proving to herself her renewed worth as a sexual and sensual woman.

Those who have read her metaphysical poetry collection, *Black Holes Within Us*, will not be disappointed. She again calls the universe into play, as both the context for her love and as providing a means for its expression. Witty and explicit, but also devoted, romantic and tender, the poems give a voice to those women who lack either the language or the courage to express and share their own experiences and emotions. Maybe the poems also encourage greater insight and self-awareness in sisters worldwide.

H/ERO/T/IC BOOK

Marta Markoska

Translated by
Aleksandra Spaseska

Proverse Hong Kong

H/ERO/T/IC BOOK
By Marta Markoska
First edition published in paperback in Hong Kong
by Proverse Hong Kong, under sole and exclusive licence
March / April 2020.
ISBN 13: 978-988-8491-96-4

Enquiries to Proverse Hong Kong
P.O. Box 259, Tung Chung Post Office,
Lantau, NT, Hong Kong SAR, China.
Email: proverse@netvigator.com;
Web: www.proversepublishing.com

Cover photo by and courtesy of Toshe Janev.
Cover design by Artist Hong Kong.

British Library Cataloguing in Publication Data
A catalogue record for the first paperback edition
is available from the British Library

THE STORY BEHIND THIS H/ERO/T/IC BOOK

I was a public figure (actually, I still am) before I decided to make the most of the difference that "public figure" status can achieve.

Before I published my first book I was a successful self-taught musician, who emerged as one of the top female musical artists in Macedonia. As the very first female percussionist in the country, I played with all the famous and respected Macedonian jazz instrumentalists and also with many international musicians.

With my academic background in literature and inspired by the many books I had devoured, I started to write intensively. As my writing career progressed, I slowly wound down my musical career to give priority to my writing. After publishing my fifth book, I was diagnosed with breast cancer, and I had a mastectomy on my right breast. After having reconstructive and several aesthetic surgeries, I felt whole again, and unexpectedly, I now feel even more confident than before. I have changed my entire lifestyle. I have become more aware of myself and more aware of my femininity – that is, more aware of what I truly am and of what I can become as a woman. Nobody, except five family members and five of my other friends knew (and in fact they still don't know) what happened to me.

As a public figure in Macedonia, I felt an enormous pressure to keep my story as confidential as I could. I wasn't prepared to tell anyone. Concurrently, while this traumatic incident was happening, I got a divorce. How it all happened still leaves me bewildered today. We were madly in love when I realized that my husband was suffering from Obsessive Compulsive Disorder (OCD) and clinical depression. He did not want to admit it or seek professional help. He became suicidal because he thought he had a brain tumour. I was so stressed and scared by the thought of what might happen to him. He cried constantly and started to act weirdly. When the man you love more than yourself constantly wants to end his life, you have no option but to vanish from this world, as well, as a self-sacrifice. When no one was here to help, I became ill. I was diagnosed with cancer resulting from two years constant overdose of stress. I said to my now ex-husband, "I can't live with your death; you will continue to live with my illness".[i] So, this was the genesis of my illness – it shows how a great love can prove cancerous, if you don't take care of your own well-being. I was literally prepared to die for him.

The surgery also added more challenges to our relationship. He wanted a baby and he was devastated to see the aftermath of my operations. He began to self-medicate on antidepressants and I witnessed how his well-being deteriorated with his worsening alcoholism. He couldn't accept my sickness and felt without hope. He did not understand the sacrifices I chose to go through for our relationship. I wanted to teach him what an unconditional love is, but he couldn't handle my misfortune; he still wanted to kill himself.[ii] He became aloof and constantly pushed me away from intimacy. He was totally drawn into depression.

Finally, I decided to get a divorce to save both of us – to spare him from suffering further and to release myself from the drama. I let him go even though he was the love of my life. I was emotionally empty. I did not have him anymore when I needed him the most. I found myself in the middle of nowhere – without a job, without my man, without love and support, and without my right breast. I even lost a few close friends, who thought my cancer was contagious. But as they say, what doesn't kill you makes you stronger. I revolutionized my lifestyle and started an intense workout routine twenty days after my mastectomy. With dedication, perseverance and motivation, I achieved the perfect body shape I have always dreamt of. While I kept silent about my illness, everyone was simply astonished at how I have transformed myself from a depressed-looking lady to a stunning, strong woman. Everyone complemented me on how I shone and how glowing my aura has become, which they have never seen in me before.

It's now more than five years since my mastectomy (28th of August, 2014) and I have never celebrated my life as greatly. The stories of Angelina Jolie, Sheryl Crow, Kylie Minogue and Anastacia have made me realize that I am not alone. They gave me hope that all is not lost. Through them, I have found the courage to share my story so that anyone who feels isolated, depressed and left alone will also find the strength to pick up the broken pieces of their selves and become whole again.

It may sound quite a story that one young poetess, a writer from a small country where everybody knows everybody, was able to keep her illness a secret for five years. But now I have realized that the privilege of strength as a strong woman should not end with me, but has to be shared with everyone else.

I know I am not an exception. I am neither the prettiest, nor the only one with this problem. But I do have a strong will to campaign for awakening, underscoring the point that a woman can still look great and desirable in spite of the intensity of the problem she has to go through. BEING A WOMAN IS A MIND SET!

As a respected public figure and a writer, I am sure that, by exposing this story of my experience, I can bring courage to many Macedonian women who are fighting the same battle and who do not have a voice in this male-dominated society. I hope my voice will go a long way to save other women's lives from complete destruction.

Although cancer may take away the opportunity to bear a child, it should not stop anyone from living and embracing their womanhood. What is more important is to bring consciousness and awareness to all women in my country and abroad that there is life after breast cancer. And that anyone can still live fully with dignity and respect.

After my previous book, *Black Holes Within Us*, which was written in the saddest period of my life, I changed my lifestyle completely and that was the beginning of my writing this H/ERO/T/IC BOOK, again, strictly from my own experiences during my period of recovery. I hope, with these materials, I can convince you that a normal, graceful life of being a woman is still possible. If I hadn't told my story above, would you ever suspect that I have been dreadfully ill?

Sincerely with Love,
Marta Markoska

H/ERO/T/IC BOOK
Marta Markoska

PURE LOVE

To Jasmin Jasaragic

The Croatian guy who unselfishly served me his time while
I was writing these poems during my recovery period

SUCK ME IN

When I breathed you in, you smelled like eternity
and I thought that we were stronger than oblivion,
not a river running and losing its trail
somewhere in the depressed depth of the tender soil.

Some day we will surge to the surface,
like all underground water does...
But it will take us quite some time
to converge again, and it is uncertain
if we will ever be the ocean
we imagined we would become.

31.07.2014

ENTER ME LIKE A ...

I wanted you to be the kernel to my walnut
lying in my armour
I wanted you to be the pearl to my shell
so I can shower you with my juices
I wanted you to be the worm to my cherry
so you can relish its sweetness

I wanted you to be the leader of my tribe
To enter me like a sprout enters the seed
To be my salvation and be my demise

And from all that
all you ever called me was
a little love emperor!

01.08.2014

TAKE ME

I don't want you to see me as chaste
it gives me a guilty conscience
preventing me from roaring my lust for you
like wild animals copulating

I don't want you to mourn me
to pity me and be sad over me
as if I am a saint sitting by Christ's knees
or Holy Mary Perybleptos[iii]

Lust for me as if you hate me
With the same strength and ferocity
Violate me as if I am your enemy
With all the hatred boiling inside you.

Take me like a sacrifice to a holy altar
Like a wolf carrying a lamb in its jaws
Take the last whiff of life from my veins
And I shall pulsate like the vein in the neck of an antelope
fallen in the mercy of a lion's clutch

Take me far away to the warm waters;
Drown me in their passion like a shell!

Take me while it's not too late, for not even the Gulf
Stream
could ever warm up what has already gone cold!

04.08.2014

RUB ME

On Sundays when the rain smells of linden
and boredom draws me to thinking of you
My left hand caresses the right
and my thighs rub against one another
in absence of someone else's touch

I need you to pull the trigger
When I remember that
We are drinking alone
We are sleeping alone

On Sundays when the rain smells of linden
and there is just one empty coffee cup on the table
a book that no one is reading anymore
keys that no longer unlock anything
memories that no one remembers anymore

I need you to pull the trigger
because we have been
Drinking alone
Sleeping alone
for far too long.

05.08.2014

POUR ME

I hide in the whiteness of a paper sheet
and within it I am changing into all the colours:
The graffiti of my heart that you don't see
and the colour pink of my coyness
are mixed with the yellow, the colour of reason,
and the blue from my ancestors' blood,
creating an aura that no painter
could ever paint
and no waters will ever wash off

13.08.2014

SPREAD ME

The sky is too narrow for the both of us
we gathered all its blessings
Now we have no home, we are nobody's children
and we thought it was God's design that we meet
not for us to double our joys
But to share our griefs

The Earth is too round
to understand the sharpness of angles
of strict geometric forms
that life had put us in
And so, trapped in multiple dimensions
we are hoping for a linear life

You say: Fate is corrupt
but She will take no pennies
And we don't have millions to bribe Her
so that we are allowed to live by each other's side
as much as we want to
as much as we deserve!

15.10.2014

MAP ME

If my body is an uncharted territory
between two parties at war
And you want to be the first one to claim it
stick a flag that says it belongs only to you
Do you think that you know how to tame it
how to take care of it, nurture it and caress it?

My body is not a terrain on a geography map
where you can proclaim yourself emperor
My body is an entire history
Where many fates are written
Where many names are signed
Passed by many conquerors
many empires have crumbled upon it
many empires bowed down before it

But my body to you is a volcano's magma
Unfriendly stratosphere with no oxygen
Unreachable rain forest with wild beasts
Stopping you from charting the map of your life
that I longed for, for so long

17.10.2014

BOIL ME

Favourable wind
from my ascendant in Gemini
makes waves to your dunes
from your ascendant in Virgo

The water from Cancer
tames your fiery emotions
and your Aries boils up
all the juices flowing through me

The two of us are a perfect symbiosis
of the four life-giving elements:
Water
Air
Earth
Fire

The stars conspired
We met to find the missing fifth – love?

18.10.2014

COUNTING MY PENNIES:
I AM THINKING HOW YOU ARE THE MOST
VALUABLE THING IN MY LIFE

When I am climbing a mountain relentlessly
what I am really thinking of
is how to conquer your peak
When I am tasting all the southern fruits
what I am really thinking of
is how I'd climb the North Pole with you

When I am straightening the curtains
what I am really thinking of
is straightening your shirt collar.

When I am turning the pages of the book you gave me
what I am really thinking of
is tracing your sides with my fingertips

When I am cooking all the meals in a day
what I am really thinking of
is tasting you and how I never stop
consuming you until you fully
melt in my mouth
and become one with my body

When I am admiring the first snow
what I am really thinking of
is how you melted the entire frost inside me
When I am watching my favourite TV show
what I am really thinking of
is how you are playing the lead role in my life
And as I clutch the remote
I am thinking you are closer to me

I bathe in the essential oils that bear your name
and I am thinking how you are slipping through my fingers

While you are gone
I write poems
I buy essential oils
I watch TV shows for hours
clutching the remote
eating southern fruits
and cooking for hours
and staring at the snow
and climbing mountains

While you are gone
I am writing a book
that I can touch
while I fall asleep
instead of you.

01.07.2015

INTERCEPT ME

I envy you how well you've mastered
writing without saying anything
I try to keep up with you
so we can communicate in detours
and never meet half way...

I envy your steadiness
restraint and classy poise
You give me no assurance that you are the one
Although you are consciously straining to convince me
in your chastity and sanctity
And we could have ruled the World
and instead of being decent
we could have roared with pleasure...
But that is my vulgarity
I am no good at lyric phrases...
I am just clumsily showing you
that I long for your caresses

03.01.2015

DESINTEGRATE ME, RECREATE ME

It is dangerous to reach into someone's magnetic field
you might burn down, turn into ashes
Get sucked into its mass
Have your atoms disintegrated
Be dissolved beyond recognition
Be swallowed into its magnetism
as if you never existed

Yet, I will reach into your magnetic field
to examine your amperage
to feel you pulsating in my hands
like a little star before it burns out

I will reach into your magnetic field
so I can map it in my experiences
that are never gained without giving many sacrifices

I surrender to your blinding energy
I allow you to break me down to subatomic particles
to reorganize the structure of my existence
to recreate me to your needs
to give me
New essence
New mass
New energy
And then, with our electric discharges
we could light up a city!

03.02.2015

COME NEAR ME

Poems are not enough
for me to bathe in them
when you're not there to stir my water
I tremble before the wait for each new line
like a delicate sheet of paper before flame

The waiting thrills every cell of my being
changing its DNA structure
with the very thought of our bodies meeting

This longing for a touch has lasted for too long
in this brief life where we don't know
where we will meet the sunset or the dawn

Don't delay our exhalations
for any future lives
where you might be the high tide and I will be – the low

Come near me and allow me to sink you like Atlantis[iv]
so I will be the only one to know where to find you again

Come near me and allow me to dock in your coves
And you, my restless sea – will rock me perpetually...

18.08.2015

I AM READY

Tonight I am prepared
to flow into your bed
to make you drink from my nectar
to tickle your feet with a whisper
while telling you stories with a sigh

I will make you climax using only words
I will awaken your animal nature
I will whisper in your ear and lick you
with the tip of my tongue like when I am tasting soup
checking if it's hot, or
when I am gently tasting a chili pepper
checking if it's hot...

Tonight I am prepared
to touch your neck
as though I am reaching across

to rub against your back
as though I couldn't get through

to lean against your hips
as though I am drunkenly slouching

to caress your bottom
as though I am putting your wallet into a pocket

to touch your hair
as though I was shaking off a leaf

to smell your skin
as though I admire your perfume...

Sometimes I lick
the pages of the book as I turn them
imagining it's you!

30.11.2015

HEAT ME

Keep me warm with your breath like when you fog the
mirror
for otherwise you wouldn't see the life
coming out of your nostrils
same as when we make love
and every lull is a disappearance
in becoming one with the other

Keep the bellybutton of my primal beginning warm
let it testify to the life inside the womb
where we learn how to receive and to recognize
love's first juices

Keep my feet warm, my feet that became rugged
while searching myself in you, that calloused while running
towards love
that bled while searching for the right mould
so they could stand straight, find a home forever

Keep the buds of my spring warm
so they can blossom and you can sense their scent
a scent only you can inspire
so you can drink their morning dew
and soften before you harden again

04.09.2016

LET ME

Be my new scientific breakthrough
so I can research you over all meridians
and dock in the cove where
all our fluids still evaporate...
So I can stir the volcano and let the magma flow out
and turn us into fossils
from where new descendants will sprout

Take me into your shores
of the abandoned and the never forgotten ones...

Be my new scientific breakthrough
allow me to measure your voltage
when you are thrillingly trembling inside me
So I can feel the earthquake while
your structure survives
the typhoon of exaltation

Take me into your experiment chambers
so we can create an electric circuit

Be my new scientific breakthrough
so I can examine you organ by organ
enter your cells
and operate in the field of your DNA
where I will try also to write myself in

Let me inside your essence
as I let you inside me
over and over again!

19.06.2016

EXPLORE ME

We entered the wheat field to examine
the alien tracks, and left our own mark
to be examined by next civilizations

We entered the field of politics
to demonstrate that blood should boil
in other parts of our bodies

We entered the field of mathematics
to calculate the sadness of goodbye
and reached a result equaling death

We also entered the field of physics
to calculate how long we could
oscillate in the same frequency of enjoyment

We entered the field of zero-point
because without gravity, the climax is greater,
And after that we become bodiless

We entered the field of all science
to understand how ignorant we are
when it comes to love and lust

We will also enter the field of history
as lovers who found all present and future times
to be too confining!

19.06.2016

STOP ME

I don't want us to become Aleppo
A pile of feelings, like a blind dog
following me year after year, limping

I don't want us to become Aleppo
I promised you heaven, like the city used to be
Smells and flavours for all senses

I don't want us to become Aleppo
After years of abundant beauty
to see only horror and ruins

I don't want us to become Aleppo
because I will be the first to become a suicide-bomber
Who will blow all your illusions about love into pieces.

15.12.2016

THE DICE ARE ROLLING, AND WERE NEVER SET RIGHT ANYWAY

You threw them in my face and said
Here, you set them,
You always wanted to arrange them
By your will, by your whim

We used to throw the dice up high
then speculate if we could
guess their total count...
As if that number could show us
how should we proceed
should we act
or forever concede

I used to believe, back then, that all was fated
And you – that all was unformulated;
I – that all is divine
And you – that all is bovine

We used to throw the dice up high
then speculate if we could
guess their total count...
As if that would show us
which one of us was right
which way to go
Should we go together
or to each their own.

Alea iacta est[v]
don't put us
to the test
on alert,
cramped up
in suspense

...

You say, let's set the dice!
But I object, for in the next second
they will be undone, just like the sheets
of a bed just made.

Here they are, up high
our dice fly once again
as if we are waiting
for them to tell the truth
for them to reveal our fate
And as they fall, the silence whispers:

Alea iacta est,
No contest,
No contest,
No contest...

16.12.2014

HOME ME

No winds could ever take away the sorrow you caused
when you stopped writing back
I have in me the joy of a memory
that we used to exist, at least on paper
that will testify longer how we hosted each other
Although we never made a home

I was spoiled by your selfless vigilance
As if I were a spiderweb in your hands
with you springing me gently – without tearing
No winter could be colder
than when you stopped writing back
Still, I will cherish the spring of our encounter
that we were all seasons to each other once
whose cycles will endure until the end of the Earth
and their concentric circles
will keep on expanding throughout Space.

02.04.2018

... AND ITS VERSIONS
(to a Few Others ...)

IMPRISON ME
PRAISE ME
RAISE ME

To G.

When your yellow tongue
collapses in my egg white
I feel a new homeland can be born

We will raise tinny fluffy bunnies
To keep our warmth
When we won't be together

I promise I won't give them your name
I'll even raise them as you raised me

I praise the moment when I'll lose my appetite
For killing bunnies to satisfy your lack of love
and compensate in your stomach

You imprisoned me like a bunny
Who didn't have anywhere to go
You were my saviour and my slaughterer
At the same time!

2016

INWARD FLOW

To G.

If I could drip in your mouth
at least one drop of menstrual blood
instead of wine, without telling you
that your soul will be ritually
initiated
infected
infested
Together we could drink up
the Red Sea
That Yahweh[vi] turned into blood
and bring back into us all the life that is draining away

And the wine...
Let's leave the wine to the beginners
for they need to drown in the shallow end many more times
before they can swim to our experiences paid for in blood!

2017

SPICED BUT CHILLED

To A.

If someone can describe your body
wrapped in a sheet
while I am trying to write
my female contours onto your manhood
others might protest and say
that I am not a creative but a selfish artist
thinking only how to put a self-note
a footnote
a sign
as if I possess your body
as a work of art, an icon;
wanting love to be immortalized
and preserved from decaying

If someone can describe your nudity
Better than me, while we are wrapped
like a taco and our sauces taste
like bitter-sweet vanishing,
then you should be someone else's sculpture,
and I…
I should be but a leaf that
accidentally covered your manhood.

2017

MENSTRUAL

Menstrualism is the new instrumentalism
Touch me gently with your nominalism
Lick me tenderly with your verbalism

Genitally comes before genetically
I am putting my Italy before your Brittany
You are putting your Mexico without an exit
Exile me on the top of your sacred hill
I'll silently sit there for centuries
Export Companies will envy us
For delivering so many babies
Foolishly in love with their parents
Making love to make more babies
They "apparently" will love them as we do

28.10.2017

REMEMBRANCE ROOM

To G.

My knees rejoice
and my hands are shaking while
as I touch your neck
I renounce you

Don't hold your breath
that titillates my cleavage
at least until we triumph
and throw the confetti

You will keep me for a long, long time
in your remembrance room
of perfect orgasms
And I consciously allowed
others to touch you
so I can write poems
that touch me

2018

QUIETLY

To D.

For some people to learn how to talk quietly
they first need to learn how to make love quietly
When they learn to caress
they will fondle with words
they will whisper in each other's ears
with no need to share grand truths
They will be satisfied with the warmth of breath
and the exchanged moisture on their bodies
the joy of the touch of hairs on their skins
and the silently secreted naked secrets

The juices of their excitement
if they could keep it in longer
will tell them they entered eternity
and that no earthly truth will ever be important to them.

Alas, if they could only learn how to make love quietly.

2018

PURPLE ME

Purple me in perpetuity
Pure like periphery skin
with all veins and drains
wanting to show through the pulse
Purify me like a purple lotus
Pamper me like a poodle
with curls, curdle me
like a clay pot in your hands
Pineapple my juices
Horn my Pipes
Blow your winds
in to my Tubes
Peach my cherry pie
with your syrup
Be my Pentagon
Make me negotiate
your intentions
Convince me that
Purple is a new Orange

2018

CORONATION

To G.

You underestimated my survival instincts
Wanted to see me crawling
Under your imaginary crown
Licking your feet, with you arguing how
You were always there when I needed
A plumber
A car mechanic
A house keeper
A dish washer

But I just needed your body
To maintain it
To worship your water-pipe
To keep your car engine on
To guard you like my home
To dine from your dishes

You underestimated my survival instincts
Me, The One who makes her partners feel like kings
For a Queen is born once in a Blue Moon.

And now we are even…
You took advantage of the first chance you got
And I proclaimed myself a Queen
Who reigns over all yet-to-be-lived opportunities!

2018

THE NEW ATLANTIS ILIAD AND ODYSSEY[vii]

To D. and I.

You both discovered me like Atlantis
so you can write all over me
Your New Odyssey
And our descendants praise us in verses
for at least a thousand years
in a newly created Iliad.

I discovered you like Atlantis
So I can call you both my New Odysseys
who are yet to fight battles with all the Danaans[viii]
for the new Iliad to have a happy ending
for at least a thousand years.

We discovered three new continents
where we can always stand
and catch a breath when life pushes us
to the edge of the shore, and the tide pulls us in deeper
We now have each other as a Holy Trinity,
three lands where we can cast our anchors
any time we feel worn out.

Let The New Era begin!

22.06.2018
(written by memory of the original from 17.06.2018)

BIOGRAPHY OF MARTA MARKOSKA

Marta Markoska was born on 29.06.1981 in Skopje, Macedonia.

She holds a Bachelor's degree in General and Comparative Literature from the "Blaze Koneski" Faculty of Philology in Skopje, and a Master's degree in Cultural Studies from the Institute of Macedonian Literature also in Skopje.

She is a member of the Writers' Association of Macedonia. Her publications to date are:

- *H/ERO/T/IC BOOK* (bilingual, Macedonian / English; erotic poetry, 2019)
- *FIL/L/M/ED STOR/I/ES*, Studies and Essays about Movies and Cinematography (2017)
- *Black Holes Within Us*, Serbian translation "Crne rupe u nama" (2017)
- *Black Holes Within Us*, 2nd Edition, Macedonian-English translation ("Todor Chalovski" Award, 2015)
- *Black Holes Within Us*, 1st Edition, Poetry Book ("Beli Mugri" Award, 2014)
- *Culture and Memory* (Book of Cultural Studies), 2014
- *A Discussion on Zen Buddhism: A Religious and Philosophical Transcendence Between Eastern and Western Thought, a Scientific Study* (2013)
- *Headfirst Toward the Heights*, Poetry (2nd Edition)
- *Headfirst Toward the Heights*, Poetry (1st Edition, Winner of the "Aco Karamanov" Award)
- Hyper Hypotheses, a Collection of Essays (2011)
- *Whirlpool in Bethlehem*, a Collection of Stories (2010)
- *All Tributaries Flow Into My Basin*, Poetry (2009).

LITERARY AWARDS

"Todor Calovski" (2015) for poetry, essays, critic and creative prose
"Nova Makedonija" (2015) for short story, 'Heights of Felix'
"Beli Mugri" (2014) for poetry book, *Black Holes Within Us*
"Aco Karamanov" (2012) for poetry book, *Headfirst Toward The Height*
"Elektrolit" (2007) for best short story, 'What happens when you're reading Frazer'

Her writings have been included in many Macedonian and foreign Anthologies, Magazines and Scientific Journals. Markoska is also an anthology maker and author of the preface of the book entitled, *Love Sailings' Reefs* (an anthology of poems dedicated to Eros and Love, 2014).

She was the pioneer in **launching** The First Literary Talk Show in Macedonia, *Literary Magnitudes*, dedicated to all famous Macedonian poets.

Markoska is also well known to the audience with her Late Night Show named, **Marta's Palace**, and for the **Campaign for showing the Beauty of a Woman After Breast Cancer** which she is launching at the very same time as publishing this book.

AUTHOR'S NOTES ON THE POEMS

[i] Subconsciously, it seems I became ill to save his life. I might have thought that my illness could be a lesson to him to see what he did to me with his constant game of push and pull.

[ii] Living in constant fear that I would lose him for ever, from jumping of the 13th floor, taking an overdose, or from (imagined) "lung cancer", I was diagnosed with breast cancer. (Read, 'Life is Cycle (Circus)' in Marta Markoska, *Black Holes Within Us*. Or, you can hear my poems at the following link: https://www.youtube.com/playlist?list=PLJ59WTjTwoFuxaj3krh HOLe6VLSgDad2E

[iii] Holy Mary Perybleptos: the Holy Mother of God Peribleptos is one of the oldest churches in the historic town of Ohrid in southwestern Macedonia. The frescoes in the church include images from the life of the Virgin Mary.

[iv] Atlantis: a fictional island in an allegory by the Ancient Greek writer and philosopher, Plato. In his work, Atlantis becomes submerged in the ocean. Later writers take it as symbolizing a lost place or a lost civilization or culture.

[v] Alea iacta est (Latin): the die are thrown.

[vi] "Yahweh": The name for "God" in the Old Testament of the Christian Bible.

[vii] *Odyssey* and *Iliad*: two works of the ancient world; the *Iliad* telling about the siege and fall of Troy and the *Odyssey* about the journey home from Troy of the Greek, Odysseus.

[viii] Danaans: a term for the ancient Greeks.

The formal shape of Marta Markoska's remarkable poems, expertly translated by Aleksandra Spaseska, contains without constraining expressions of obsessive love – love intense, explicit, articulate, imaginative, exploratory – conceived in the ambiguity which is both art and life itself.

—Gillian Bickley
Author of *For the Record, Moving House, Sightings, China Suite, Perceptions* (Proverse Hong Kong, 2003, 2005, 2007, 2009, 2012)

This edgy collection of poetry is simultaneously empowering, provocative and unexpectedly wistful. Marta Markoska slashes naked emotion bare, coupling it with the true physicality of need. She explores themes of feminism, abandonment, the dissipation of desire and desire itself.

Her poetry collectively becomes a tactile tale of longing, need, urgency, hurt, wild abandon, pleasure, self-doubt and quiescence. Throughout, erotica merges with psychological self-examination to elicit some quite fascinating insights. The poet draws on scientific, geological, mathematical and astronomical metaphor, making for an intelligent discourse within a subjective realm.

A bold read – shocking in honesty and pleasurable in excellence.

—Hayley Ann Solomon
author of *Celestial Promise* and *Under the Shade of the Feijoa Trees* (Proverse Hong Kong, 2017, 2018; Proverse Supplementary Prize Winner, 2016, 2017)

ADVANCE COMMENT
on the English version of Marta Markoska's
H/ERO/T/IC BOOK,
published by Proverse Hong Kong in March / April 2020
Written <u>before</u> reading Markoska's introductory essay,
'The Story Behind This H/ERO/T/IC BOOK'

The extent to which one knows a subject is perhaps best measured by the way one describes it. And how one describes it provides an opportunity to learn for those who are new to the subject, as well as for those who thought they were already well versed in it.

Markoska knows her subject, physical intimacy. Her poems unearth it, open it up, stare into it. It is not only about biology, but also about bodies, bodies-in-space, therefore land rights, geography, territory, ancestry. Her poetry turns intimacy into a primal wonder, making us ask why we had never thought of ourselves in this way. Your body is always greater than you, more expansive, much older, and wiser too. In a poem of hers:

"…My body is an entire history
Where many fates are written
Where many names are signed
Passed by many conquerors
many empires have crumbled upon it
many empires bowed down before it"

Physical intimacy cannot do without bodies. But bodies cannot always be equated with intimacy. In one poem about her body, Markoska sees it as an instrument of pleasure, not just for herself, but for the universe itself to touch, an instrument for the female gender to recreate manhood – again and again in each act of sex. And she juxtaposes the "humanity-creating" – although seemingly selfish – sexual pleasures which her body can endow with many sterile erotic art forms of bodies:

"If someone can describe your body
wrapped in a sheet
while I am trying to write
my female contours onto your manhood..."

Woven into her poetry are both philosophy and wisdom, each of which is essential for humanity to re-vision sexual experience. The titles of the poems are tabloid-sensual and this may be anathema to many. But each poem certainly has the power to awaken in us the deeply buried divine wisdom of the original and authentic functioning of the human body.

—Elbert Siu Ping Lee
author of *Rain on the Pacific Coast* (Proverse, 2013)

ADVANCE COMMENTS

on the English version of Marta Markoska's
H/ERO/T/IC BOOK,
published by Proverse Hong Kong in March / April 2020
Written <u>after</u> reading Markoska's introductory essay,
'The Story Behind This H/ERO/T/IC BOOK'

In lyrical language, Markoska works her love of words into expressions of love, lust, desire, tenderness and savagery within the sphere of physical intimacy. She explores closeness and loss, rapture and pain through exciting and surprising imagery. A celebration of the body eclectic.

—Joy Al-Sofi
    a Proverse Poetry Prize winner, 2016

Poems with a palpable sense of passion which flips between love and hate, between hectoring and urging on the beloved, between repairing the breach and declaring the breach a necessary part of the exchange. Lyrics which are almost over-the-top but exhibit enough restraint to complete their ritualistic impetus: to exorcize as well as to celebrate.

—Andrew Simpson Guthrie
    author of *Alphabet* (Proverse 2015;
    an International Proverse Prize Finalist, 2013)

SOME POETRY AND POETRY COLLECTIONS
Published by Proverse Hong Kong

Alphabet, by Andrew S. Guthrie. 2015.

Astra and Sebastian, by L.W. Illsley. 2011.

Bliss of Bewilderment, by Birgit Bunzel Linder. 2017.

The Burning Lake, by Jonathan Locke Hart. 2016.

Celestial Promise, by Hayley Ann Solomon. 2017.

Chasing light, by Patricia Glinton Meicholas. 2013.

China suite and other poems,
by Gillian Bickley. 2009.

Epochal Reckonings,
by J.P. Linstroth. 2020. (Scheduled)

For the record and other poems of Hong Kong,
by Gillian Bickley. 2003.

Frida Kahlo's cry and other poems,
by Laura Solomon. 2015.

Heart to Heart: Poems, by Patty Ho. 2010.

H/ERO/T/IC BOOK, by Marta Markoska. 2020.

Home, away, elsewhere,
by Vaughan Rapatahana. 2011.

Immortelle and bhandaaraa poems,
by Lelawattee Manoo-Rahming. 2011.

In vitro, by Laura Solomon. 2nd ed. 2014.

Irreverent poems for pretentious people,
by Henrik Hoeg. 2016.

The layers between (essays and poems),
by Celia Claase. 2015.

Of leaves & ashes, by Patty Ho. 2016.

Life Lines, by Shahilla Shariff. 2011.

*Mingled voices: the international Proverse Poetry Prize
anthology 2016*, edited by Gillian and Verner Bickley. 2017.

*Mingled voices 2: the international Proverse Poetry Prize
anthology 2017*, edited by Gillian and Verner Bickley. 2018.

*Mingled voices 3: the international Proverse Poetry Prize
anthology 2018*, edited by Gillian and Verner Bickley. 2019.

*Mingled voices 4: the international Proverse Poetry Prize
anthology 2019*, edited by Gillian and Verner Bickley. 2020.
(Scheduled)

Moving house and other poems from Hong Kong,
by Gillian Bickley. 2005.

Over the Years: Selected Collected Poems, 1972-2015,
by Gillian Bickley. 2017.

Painting the borrowed house: poems,
by Kate Rogers. 2008.

Perceptions, by Gillian Bickley. 2012.

Poems from the Wilderness, by Jack Mayer. 2020. (Scheduled)

Rain on the pacific coast,
by Elbert Siu Ping Lee. 2013.

refrain, by Jason S. Polley. 2010.

Savage Charm, by Ahmed Elbeshlawy. 2019.

Shadow play, by James Norcliffe. 2012.

Shadows in deferment, by Birgit Bunzel Linder. 2013.

Shifting sands, by Deepa Vanjani. 2016.

Sightings: a collection of poetry, with an essay, 'communicating poems', by Gillian Bickley. 2007.

Smoked pearl: poems of Hong Kong and beyond, by Akin Jeje (Akinsola Olufemi Jeje). 2010.

Of symbols misused, by Mary-Jane Newton. 2011.

The Hummingbird Sometimes Flies Backwards, by D.J. Hamilton. 2019.

The Year of the Apparitions, by José Manuel Sevilla. 2020 (*Scheduled*)

Unlocking, by Mary-Jane Newton. March 2014.

Violet, by Carolina Ilica. March 2019.

Wonder, lust & itchy feet, by Sally Dellow. 2011.

FIND OUT MORE ABOUT OUR AUTHORS, BOOKS, EVENTS AND LITERARY PRIZES

Visit our website: http://www.proversepublishing.com
Visit our distributor's website: www.cup.cuhk.edu.hk

Follow us on Twitter
Follow news and conversation: twitter.com/Proversebooks
OR
Copy and paste the following to your browser window and follow the instructions: https://twitter.com/#!/ProverseBooks

"Like" us on www.facebook.com/ProversePress

Request our free E-Newsletter
Send your request to info@proversepublishing.com.

Availability
Available in Hong Kong and world-wide
from our Hong Kong based distributor,
The Chinese University of Hong Kong Press,
The Chinese University of Hong Kong,
Shatin, NT, Hong Kong SAR, China.
Email: cup@cuhk.edu.hk.
Website: www.cup.cuhk.edu.hk.
All titles are available from Proverse Hong Kong,
http://www.proversepublishing.com
From many online retailers, including amazon.com,
amazon.co.uk, and others.

Stock-holding retailers
Hong Kong (CUHKP, Bookazine)
Canada (Elizabeth Campbell Books),
Andorra (Llibreria La Puça, La Llibreria).

Orders may be made from bookshops
in the UK and elsewhere.

Ebooks
Most of our titles are available also as Ebooks.